# Lockdown Lamentations

### – A Poem Collection -

**By RAN SEVERIN**

## GAME ON

They play us

Game on

You and I shrivel in fear

Game on

 You accuse your neighbor

Game on

Forgetting to love your neighbor like yourself

Game on

 You're scared of me

Game on

While I'm scared of you

Game on

 Forgetting to love my neighbor like myself

Game on

 I don't know

Game on

If you're one of them

Game on

Stirring up hate against me and mine

Game on

While you're scared

Game on

I'm one of them

Game on

Stirring up hate against you and yours

Game on

They play us

Game on

We are the majority

Game on

Shrivel ling in fear of the few

Game on

## 1939

I wasn't there in 1939

Or was I?

Suddenly I understand

Eerie insight revealed

Through my eyes, through my soul, through my spirit

I see fear being injected strategically and in abundance

Roaring storms of slickly produced propaganda

Sweeping our shores and souls

Disguised as "News"

The masses flooded and drowned by relentless campaigns, endless streams of contaminated noise

Calculated pretence from friendly- looking well groomed servants of darkness

Pretending to care about good kind people

Or maybe not so good kind people

Hardworking "Normal" -labeled people

Believing normal is normal

Blindly convinced, there's a certain type of order to life

As they know it

Smugly content to conduct life

In an orderly manner

Taught by their father's fathers

Now

Suddenly thrust into thinking with own hearts, souls and spirits

Can they?

Will they?

Dare they swap normal for humane

Are they scared?

No —they're scared alright

Perceiving

Distant hollow cries in their hearts, souls and spirits

Are they listening?

Why switch off the convenient, soothing lies?

Too used to normal

At any cost, by any means

Are all humans worth humanity anyway?

Longing for normality will they turn a blind eye?

Yet again

Just like in 1939

## Divoc 91

Covid 19

I rebuke you

Depart

Leave

Stop the deceit

You're not even real

No matter how many times repeated

You

Are

Not

Real

Your Masters are sunken souls

Plunged into deep darkness

Lost souls

Snared

By false promises

Of Incomprehensible

Wealth and power

In exchange

For love and kindness

And a soul

We will not receive you

Or your net of destruction

Frantically cast over us

You

Are

Not

Real

Be gone

Our prayers

Abundant frequencies of loving vibrations

Will

Destroy

You

And

Your wicked Masters


## Lies


Oh the lies!

The lies make me sick

Make me ill

Make my spirit fold

Ruthless lies sprayed on me

On all of us

Persistently

Relentlessly

Consistently

Egging us on

Swaying us

Convincing us

We have to fear one another

We must stay frozen in trembling fear

Snitch on our neighbors

Await an award

For snitching on loved ones, friends, colleagues

People we used to care about or secretly resented

No civil rights left

Applauded

If

And

When

We willfully snitch on our brothers and sisters

It's the new Right

The new Good

The new Decent

The New Normal

Inflicting pain like it's no longer a moral offence

"To save Lives"

To save lies

Informed by apathetic informers

 Snitch on everyone who don't line up

Or click their heels

Become a true hero

Hero of darkness, filth and wickedness

In high places

You'll be on the winning team

 Everyone else are sore losers

With contempt for fellow humans and their well beings

Obviously

## Hitler Said

Hitler said

We are strong

And you said YES!

Hitler said

We are united

And you said YES!

Hitler said

We will help each other

And you said YES!

Hitler said

Let us be a Kingdom

And you said YES!

Hitler said

We will overcome

And you said YES!

Hitler said

We will move like one force, one people

And you said YES!

Hitler said

We have a common enemy

And you said YES!

Hitler said

It is the Jews

And you said YES!

Hitler said

The Jews want to destroy us

And you said YES!

Hitler said

We have to protect our Kingdom

And you said YES!

Hitler said

We have to unite against the enemy

And you said YES!

Hitler said

Our enemies are the Jews

And you said YES!

The Covid 19 Prop Master said

We have to destroy the enemy

And you said YES!

Tell us what to do Mein Fuehrer

Who is our enemy?

Who do you want us to destroy?

# Critical Minds

You see

It is different for us

It was always different for us

We had to comprehend or die

Physically or emotionally

Or both

We were schooled in a parallel universe

In a parallel sphere

Even when we were right there

Amongst you

We had to pick up

Fast

We had to understand

That all we were ever taught

All that surrounded us

The "Truth"

The pleasant spoken voices of the mainstream media

The guidelines for right and wrong

Rules & regulations

Set out in life

Didn't include us

Didn't encompass us

Even when we were right there with you

We found ourselves excluded

Laws, norms, guidelines

Didn't apply to us

Even when we were right there with you

Amongst you

And you didn't care

You accepted this as normal

While we were suffering

Silently

Openly

But through your callous underestimation of us

We were taught a lesson of invaluable proportion

Dwarfing fine education bought by blood money

It taught us to be critical

To be observant

To be on edge

Not to trust

To comprehend the meaning of true love

Deceit was fed to each and every one of us

Outcasts by default

Through the News

The mainstream media, the laws of the land, the rules

We involuntarily

Developed thick skins

Distrust

And sometimes

Criminal minds

We learned to decipher

We learned to discern

We learned to trust our souls, hearts, spirits and God

Not the mainstream media

Bought by blood money

We already knew

It was a lying liar

We were forced

From a very young age

To distrust

To cut through the crap

The noise

And see

What was really going on?

You gave us an advantage

An education

In critical thinking

Bet you didn't see that coming

You totally miscalculated that aspect

Like you miscalculated bringing over the strongest, most intelligent, most resilient Negroes

To your shores

But here we are now

Collectively and universally aware

Worldwide

On edge

United in love and distrust

That's why we don't accept your lies

About Covid 19

Or anything else

Really

We know better

Than to trust you blindly

Our history, our past and our present

Has guided us to this revelation

We know you're up to something foul

Entirely different and remote from the truth

You claim to share

Something sinister and soul destroying

Yet again

## Plastic

Plastic life is not important

People are

People we love

Are important

Plastic life isn't

Façade is suddenly not so up market

Jokes are on you

If you try to maintain it

Nobody buys it

The seams come apart

There's no point

Just embrace

What's here and present

Real

Reality like you never knew it

Everything stripped

Down

To

It's raw

Base

You're vulnerable now

Can't hide in plastic

You're called out

Plastic is out

Reality is in

Can you hang?

Can you embrace reality?

Your façade was impeccable

Now laughable

Pitiful and full of infected cracks

Can you connect?

With what's left?

A soul screaming in the distance

A soul yearning to be connected

Can you hear it?


## Imagine


Imagine living in a world

Where

White people were called names

Like

Evil, white devil, peeled potato, white pig, wicked, white Satanist

Dimwit, halfwit, icky white, low-life white, soulless white, left foot white

Cold white, ice white, white murderer, smelly white, heartless white, unsophisticated white

Bland white, devil white, white thief

Or

Worse

A world where white people were disproportionally incarcerated

Always suspected

Of crimes

Not conceived nor carried out

Always stopped and checked

For any graspable violation

Real

Or imagined

Where white people were mainly on the news

Due to their laziness, inability to get

Or hold a job

Their lack of ingenuity or resources

Their incapacity to dig themselves out

And up

To our standards and civil way of life

Imagine witnessing their huge bellies from generational malnutrition

And a host of pharmaceutical, experimental drugs and vaccines

Shown mercilessly in ads interrupting our idyllic evening snack

With our delightful cups of tea or coffee

Imagine a display of

 Endless crimes and drug use

Stabbings

White on white murders

Implying a lack of willingness to help or respect them selves

Always poor

Under educated

Under stimulated

Always under

Rioting, disorderly conducting and protesting

Claiming their lives somehow matter

Just imagine

But no

We can't imagine that

We're kind, compassionate, civil, decent, loving people

Our higher-ranking humanity

And superior emotional intelligence and empathy

Will not allow us

To copy nor repeat

## Equal

We're all equal now

Beautiful sentiment

Midway through the terrorizing of us

We're all equal

We're all in jail

But we're all equal

Stripped of our civil rights

Not allowed to drive to our second home

As if we had a second home

Or even a home at all

We're all equals now

Scotland's Chief Medical Advisor

Agreed

As she advised her people

They were no longer allowed

To drive

To their second home

The beach

The valleys

The hills

The mountains

Or anywhere

While she sped off to Fife

With her family

To her second home

Not once

But twice

She said "Sorry"

That she'd made a "Mistake"

Willfully, knowingly, happily

Not a bad decision

But just a mistake

Pleading for empathy

From the very people

She just instructed with unwavering sternness and theatrical concern

Claiming

We're all equal now

We're all in this together

## Freedom of Speech

I do not accept Covid 19

No raging pandemic at large

But a seasonal flu

Which most of the world

Experience

Every year

Statistically

Up to half a million people

Die in the UK

Every single year

Every

Single

Year

Sad for sure


But never highlighted, lamented on open screens

Till now

Never announced before

Citizen death tolls blasted via main stream media

On a daily basis

Why now?

Why not last year?

Or the year before?

Or the year before the year before?

Peculiarly alarming

Nonsensical

Doesn't add up

Because it doesn't add up

Civil rights snatched away

Under the pretence of worrying

About our health

But you never normally care about our health

Squeezing the life out of nurses, care home workers, teachers, social workers, single mums

With outrageous work hours

And grotesque minimal pay

So why now?

Coerced to play along

With your

Carefully constructed script

and

Your propaganda Masters' baseless "Facts"

Yet

I'm the one

Inhumane, selfish and irresponsible

If I don't comply

And not you

Who just imposed fascism with a straight face

And all it took was

 One measly week

In one week

You managed

To make people dance to your tune

Submitting to your demands

Testing obedience levels

You gleefully observed how people

Were suddenly willing to

Abandon

Their elders

Leaving them baffled and confused

In the midst of their utmost fragility

In their homes

By themselves

At the very end of their lives

Having trustfully spend their entire lives and energy

Assuming someone

Would maybe care for them

In their newfound vulnerable state

Not so

The elderly were sacrificed first

Presumed easy targets

Not having the strength to fight back

While loved ones were forbidden

To care for them

Cruelty suddenly equaled kindness

As the perpetrators claimed they so deeply cared for us all

Suggesting

We are all contagious

And need to stay apart

Because we love each other so much

Right?

I do not believe in Covid 19

I believe in an entirely different agenda

Pulled over us

Step by step

Move by move

Orchestrated

Like a military drill

If I don't play along

I'm the bad guy

Those who don't play along

Are the bad guys too

And who wants to be the bad guy?

It takes immense courage and strength

To carry that title

Especially when it doesn't even fit

I spoke up nevertheless

Within a group

Otherwise representing freedom, unity and justice

A Union group

Where I felt safe

And was part

Till I spoke up

About the narrative I was served

Suggesting another agenda might be at play

Was a little anxious to share

But convincing myself

I was in a safe space

Amongst progressive people with open minds

That was before

I was banned, expelled, shunned, rejected

Removed

Imagine the implications

In wider society

If fear wins


## Running


It's confirmed

With spirit aching clarity

 All the people I was running away from

All my life

Are running the world

Imagine all the deaths

Throughout the world

Were announced

Every day

By mainstream media

Every single day

Every hour

Every moment

Throughout the day and night

Non stop

Inconceivably absurd

Yet

Announcements of people dying

From

The common cold or flu

Are numbered and announced

Drama infested Lockdown style

Every day

Every moment

Throughout the day or night

Rolling down TV screens nationwide

Worldwide

Like raindrops making their final destination

Sliding down silently

Void of regret, mercy or discretion

Mainstream media death tolls

Unashamedly

Replace deaths from

The common cold and flu, cancer, heart attacks, strokes, car fatalities

With Covid 19 deaths

Inconceivably devious

 Eerily constructed manipulation

All the people I was running away from

All my life

Are running the world

 Now I finally understand

Why I've been running

**Nevertheless**

You don't really need much in Life

Except

A good relation with God

Thank you Covid 19

For teaching us all

Humility, gratitude and appreciation

Your intent

Was to spread fear, confusion and anxiety

You managed to do just that

Happy with your achievement?

But you miscalculated

The benefits we discovered

Along the journey

Choking in your cold iron grip

The beauty of sharing quality time

With loved ones

Whether at hand, close or afar

Suddenly appreciative for the mere act of shopping

Like never before

Helping each other carry groceries

Cooking and sharing meals

Never tasted this good

You made us realize

We're all one

We're the people

Not you

People power is powerful

We're not clacking or clapping mindlessly and obediently

For the NHS and healthcare workers

You so suddenly appreciate and cherish

And treated like worthless

Not that long ago

Do you really think

We forgot or didn't notice?

We see you

We know you're not that bothered

Shamelessly underpaid those same people

Stretched them

Till breaking point

And out of shape

Till now

You recklessly count on people being scared

Stupid

You perceive us as stupid and scared

Sheep

Blindly following

And yes

We were scared

As you came at us hard

With an unimaginable Goebbels- like assault

But your script

Lacks continuity

Cracks appear

Your carefully constructed story doesn't add up

The prop-masters failed

Don't think we noticed?

We did

Were calling you out

On social media

And now you're censoring free speech

On social media

Silencing critics

Strangling questions

Revealing your wicked scheming

And plotting

Mark my words

We the people

Will win

Nevertheless

## God help us

God help us

They're killing people

God help us

They're scaring us

They're scarring us

To death

With their relentless onslaught

Of "News"

Humming out numbers of deaths

Continuously

Where do the numbers come from?

From whence?

Do we get to check if the numbers add up?

Where do we go to check if the numbers add up?

We perceive they don't add up

They just keep on

Keeping on

Scaring us

Making us sick with fear

Our immune systems

Fail

Because of fear

And yet they just keep on scaring us

Making us sick

Even when we were not sick

To begin with

Now we're worried

Suddenly detecting symptoms

And panic

And call the ambulance

And go to the hospital

And we're scared

We're scarred

And we get weaker

And we

Die

"My people are destroyed for the lack of knowledge"

God help us all

## Still Life

Love this still life

So peacefully peace filled

In the midst of ruthless crudeness

Inhumane scheming

And plotting

To lock us all down

Keeping us captive

In technology prisons

Watched

Surveilled

Censored

Monitored

Restricted

Controlled

Doesn't face me

I love still

Still life entices me

Betters me

Makes me grateful

For what I do have

I can meditate

Draw nearer to God

My family

Learn

What I really need to learn

Listen

Be still

Be taught

Through glorious angel whispers

Overriding

The fear mongering bloodthirsty

Mass media

Doesn't face me

I know

They

Can't

And never will overpower

Nor

Beat

The Creator of the Universe

## The crime of sunbathing

Saw a sign in the park

Had to move closer

Moved closer to get a good look

To understand

What I couldn't quite comprehend

As I looked in bewilderment and disbelief

At the police sign

Did I miss something?

Are the police not those guys?

Who protect us?

From

Violence, crimes and various evils

Are the police not those guys?

To whom

We pay part of our salaries

Through taxes

Are the police not those guys

Who are there for us?

The good decent people

Respectful people

Feeling uneasy and nauseous

By the very thought

Of crossing into criminal territory and activity

As we meticulously strive

To be good people and citizens

Have the rules of engagement taken a turn?

Would appear so

As

Decency suddenly became indecent over night

I am coerced to believe

You still care about me

Wish to protect me

From the common flu

For crying out loud

Fancifully labeled Covid 19

As if to make it less common

Than the common flu

I should trust you to do the job of your Masters

Who back up their claims with numbers

Far from reality

Endlessly pouring in

Cementing the imminent danger

Of a merciless killer

So potent

It's now

Illegal to sunbathe

I will be considered a criminal if I sunbathe

In the park

You said so

With your police sign

I must not sunbathe

Or I breach the rules

And could get fined

For my crime

I'm a criminal if I sunbathe

In God's glorious sunshine

He provided freely and abundantly

To strengthen my immune system

Heal and nourish me

I'm a criminal if I play a social game

Like tennis or football

Could get fined

For this new crime

Who are we serving?

Who's going to protect us now?

## Banned

Banned today

From a Union Whatsapp group

Hit me like a violent avalanche

Unexpectedly erupted

Ferociously accumulating treacherous momentum

Flesh soul and mind

Pierced by invisible poisonous darts

Leaving me numb, furious

Frightened

By potential ramifications

Caught with evidence

Birthed by my alleged crime

Opposition against the fear mongering mass media's relentless

Onslaught of information

That is misinformation

Designed

With the sole intent

To stop me thinking clearly

Stop me listening to the voice messenger within

Make me retract, recoil

In utter fear

I posted a post

A dying tree

Just like me

Impacted by radiation from 5G

Halfway crumbling and fading

The parallel world of information juxtaposed with mains stream media

Says people are locked down

So masts can get put up

Imposing

60 Giga Hertz radiations

Threatening to obliterate trees along with the nation

While the Puppet Masters distractingly shout

Watch out for Covid 19!

Couldn't foresee the trap I so readily fell into

Or could I?

Was I an undercover rebel on a mission

Fighting on the frontlines of truth?

Or should I have listened to stomach voice jitters

Alerting me of danger?

Foolishly thinking I was in a safe space

With likeminded progressives

Eager to uphold sanity, morality and freedom

Instead

I was banned, removed, rejected, discharged

Like a pariah

Grabbed by the throat

Like a snake

About to have its teeth venom squeezed

I was the messenger

Who got shot

To save the purity of the group

 Pre-lockdown

Composed of revolutionaries

 Freedom fighters

 Unwaveringly upholding values

Securing fairness

Fighting oppression from

Sneering Masters with no time for peasants

Not this time

I was banned for freedom of speech

In a safe space

That turned out unsafe

Banned, removed, rejected, shunned and discharged

By Union Reps

Conferring and plotting behind my back

In secret

Fascism crept into the space

Like a deadly cancer cell

Invaded this place of freedom

Created to ensure unity

And combat attempts of oppression

Instead

I was banned, rejected, shunned, removed

For the greater good of the group

Think I knew

Deep down

It was all but a safe space




## Icke's take


Never heard of David Icke before

Apart from lose chatter in the distance

Affirming his status as an outcast, a conspiracy theorist

With strange obscure ridiculous laughable views

But my beloved sister

Send me a video

His "Part I Covid 19" Interview

Tuned in

Got blown away

Discombobulated

By his effortless dissemination and detangling

Of

The Master's Covid 19 script

Sneaked in and forced upon us

Waited feverishly

Till

"Part II" finally followed

My my my

Eloquent

Coherent

Impressive

Humane

Compassionate

Nothing short of a revelation

To watch

During this particular vulnerable moment in time and space

Where light equals life

Encouraging

You and I

To get involved

And do something

Anything

If not for us

Then at least for the children and the children's children

Left to grow up

Finding themselves

Involuntary part takers

In the midst of a dystopian nightmare

Of unfathomable proportions

Run, infused and injected with control, restrictions, surveillance

And fear

"Do something"

Icke urged

Make a difference

Contribute

To this world

Where freedom is still in reach

Still an option

Oppose a life in physical, moral, spiritual chains

Do it for the children

I heard

Him say

And I listened


## Virtues


Exhausting

To live in a world

Where love and kindness

Are exquisite virtues

In dire need of chasing

Excruciatingly painful to uphold

Dangerous to pursue

Rare gems

Delicate treasures

For the chosen few

How is it reality?

People so void of human sophistication

Human comprehension

Unknowledgeable in beauty of humanity affairs

The very concept of being humane

Are allowed to rule, manipulate, dictate?

Why are we not further on in our humane pursuit

In our evolved human development?

In humanity?

Inhumanity still rules

We're choking

While the caretakers of this world

Run it with

Violence, fear and unspeakable crimes

Towards humans

Enforced

By humans

Who exactly

Want this?

But a few sick twisted souls with power and funds

To script and direct the whole injured world

Can we just asphyxiate this plaque?

And not go along

Comply

With fear and submission?

We're more than those few

Once that version of reality is grasped

By the many

It will no longer be scary

At all

To do

The right thing

Every time

And change this grim world

Into a place of glory, light and true beauty

Brimming with virtues

Of which the highest are

Kindness and love

Leading to

The ultimate transition

Into

The Real New World Order

## George Floyd on my mind

How long?

When will you be humane?

When will your blood thirst end?

Why are you soulless?

Robotic

Mechanic

Cold

How long do we have to suffer

Your schizophrenic antics?

One minute

You want to kill us

Control us, eradicate us, torture us

The next

You admire and envy us

Want to copy

Our cool

Snatching our culture

Pretending you invented it

Who are you?

Why are you inhumane and void of reasoning?

Who are you?

You want to control us

 Everyone and everything around you

Who are you?

What made you

Inhumane, soulless and cold?

Will you ever change?

Why don't you want to change?

Haven't you caused enough pain?

What do you want?

Why are you copying us non-stop?

You kill us, you copy us, you kill us some more

You copy us, you envy us

You kill us

Emotionally, physically, spiritually

Then you copy us

And want us to be pals

While you keep oppressing us

Killing us, hurting us

Maiming us, torturing us

Then you want to move like us

Talk like us, dance like us

And then you want to beat us, kill us

What's wrong with you?

We pity you

In the midst of our trials

We're sick of you

So indescribable sick of you

And yet we forgive you

Again and again

We're still willing to forgive you

Do you even grasp what that says?

About us

About you

Can you stop already

Try to be humane

Try at least

Live and let live

Earn a soul

Let peace and love

Be your master

Finally

and

Forever


## Little


Little people with little power

Abominable and crippling

If they cross your path

Little spineless creatures with oh so low self esteems

With a little power

Are debilitating

If they cross your path

See you shine

They abhor that shine

They want it

They want to shine

Like you shine

They will try their hardest

To take it off you

With the little power they have

Little, little, little

They're little

Their little spirits are choked and starved

They don't like to see you shine

They want your light

They'll come for you

Claim your light

With whatever ammunition

They have at hand

Little, little, little

They're little in spirit and soul

They envy you

Because you're real and spirit filled

Soulful, authentic, real

Watch out

They're coming for you

The little, little, little

Spiritually hideous

Spineless people

## Reflect

Reflect, rethink, reset

Popped into my spirit

On my daily walk

Sweet spirit -whispering blessings

Now is the time to be still

"And know I am God"

This is the time

To be

And to be grateful

Evaluate

What you have

What you need

Grateful for what I have

My child

My siblings

My family

My peace

My stillness

A place to call home

Food

Appreciation of mundanity

In all its simple glory

 Exquisite blessings

Right here, right now

Enough

"Tomorrow will take care of itself"

Today I'm grateful


## Normality


Authority managed to insist

 Abnormal is normal

Introduced abnormal as being perfectly normal

Regardless of how abnormal

Abnormality is now absorbed as being normal

Because the authorities say so

Abnormal normal

Means

Anything is possible

Absence of morals

Now equals

Right and normal

Abnormal

 Rules

A hospital suddenly becomes

A perfectly disguised slaughter house

Where people are treated to die

Not to live

With death tolls rising and rising

Eagerly blasted through the mass media

Round the clock

Inconceivable

Impossible to conceive

But

Did people forget

When an Anti Christ reigned

Those marked out as evil human beings

Creators and instigators of destruction

Were marked

By law

With

A yellow star?

## Forced vaccine

I am all for a forced vaccine

A compulsory injection

Where breaking in and dragging out

Is a must

A necessity

It's about time we all take full responsibility

And rid ourselves of this deadly disease

This plaque of disastrous proportions

Once and for all

By all and any means

Do snitch on your neighbor

Cause

You'll be a hero

Weed them out

Single them out

Smoke them out

Ban them from our noble society

Make sure they cannot shop, travel, work

Or interact

Intersect, intervene

Be among us at all

We are all in this together

And

We

Will

Beat

This

I am all for a forced vaccine

If its components

Are made of

Peace, harmony, kindness, compassion, integrity and

Love

## Cool dude

Today

I got a smile

From a cool dude

Jogging in the park

Felt so good

For a split second

I felt connected

 To humanity

Again

The dude didn't make an exaggerated effort

To uphold

Social distancing

Neither did I

In fact

I made a deliberate move

To avoid social distancing

A new word

Synonymous

With fascism

I moved

Into his space

Into his presence

And he saw it

Acknowledged it

Embraced it

Smiled at me

For a brief moment in time

We were brothers or sisters

In sync

We were close

On the same page

We were one

Smiling at each other

Because

We appreciated

The uniqueness

Of the moment

We exchanged peace, kindness and love

In that moment

And knew

Humanity

Depends

On people

Like us

## Reflect Rethink Reset II

Reflect rethink reset

Together as one

The world we run

Reflect rethink reset

Together as one

The world we run

Reflect rethink reset

Together as one

The world we run

We are one

We ARE one

We are ONE

We are so many more than the few

Who play chess with us

And our lives

Our livelihoods

Moving us from field to field

Check mating us

For a sick kick

A game of control

Power

They are not of us

Or with us

Or for us

They are alien to humanity

Not humane

Or for humanity

Their game runs down power trip lane

They want to control us

Because they are lost

And out of control

Poisonous creatures

With

Infested scabs of insecurity and impotence

Trading humanity for money

To feel powerful

Power hungry boys with mummy issues

Disguised as men

Reflect rethink reset

Together as one

The world

We run

Together as one

We will run them out

**Two meters**

C'mon people

Wake up

Two meters distance?

Like we are all suddenly infected with Ebola

Oh word

Ebola only killed black and brown people

Not one single white person

Not even one

Funny enough

But not really funny in the slightest

How does a pandemic

Choose its victims

Like it has an agenda

To erase only specifically chosen people

Wake up people

Don't look away now

As if it has got nothing to do with you

This time it has

Everything to do with you

We are all in this together, remember?

A pandemic is impartial

No?

No, not Ebola, not AIDS or even this one

This is the big one

That takes down everyone

And black and brown people

A little more

As per usual

Are you not questioning what's happening yet?

Will you be sheep led to slaughter?

Without a sound?

Will you exercise your freedom of speech?

And speak up

Will I?

Wake up people

Even Eamon  Holmes

Bless him

Questions the narrative

Does that not make you sit up and listen?

When a treasured, polished, darling mainstream presenter

Breaks through the wall of silence and fear

Are you out there people?

Are there not more of us?

Thinking

The same?

Wake up people!

Are you out there people?

Let's unite

Form an army of resistance

We are powerful in numbers

Don't look away now

Not now, not again

History can't repeat itself

Again

We are one

Let us stand up as one

And refuse

To be manipulated, controlled, lied to

We can beat this as one

Why on earth resist?

Please don't let fear defeat you

Let's do the right thing

This is our chance to make history

To define humanity

## Just like Truman

In these times of uproot

And dire isolation

Where democracy turned into fascism

Overnight

I wonder

Exactly when

 The control and manipulation of our thoughts

Began

And how far back it goes?

Youth always rebels

From generation to generation

We rebelled as youths

We sensed

Something was off

And not in our favor

For a brief moment in time

We made noise

Like the youth before us and the youth before

We knew we were being manipulated

Kept in line

For an agenda

Removed from humanity

And human interaction

We didn't want to fit in

But had nowhere to go

Eventually

We faded out

Got caught up

Even if the rebel inside was never laid to rest

Once fiercely resisting control and manipulation

We got overcome

With doubt, fear and endless bills

We faded out

Waiting for the next fresh bash of rebels to lead the way

We couldn't have dreamt up the extend of manipulation and control

Waiting ahead to consume and frighten us

We didn't grasp the scope back then

We still don't

Albeit misfits of yesterday

With rebel hearts

Now we know

We were right all along

Now we know

We were never obstinate, difficult or crazy

We were up against dark forces

Now more sinister than ever

Blatantly disregarding humanity

Human rights

Civil liberties

Disguising their mission

Pretending to care about our health

While suffocating us in a worldwide lockdown

We need to rummage our souls

Bring out the former combat gear

And join the war for humanity

Yet again

Fight fear in search of love

Just like Truman

# God's plan

Wish I will still be around

When the world has finally transformed

Into a place of pure love

Where no-one is made to feel dirty or lesser

Based on lack of accumulated wealth

And finances

Where it's not possible to be broke

Because everyone has enough

Where women are worshipped and appreciated

For their never ending

Spirit of love

And where anyone wanting to control others

Are frowned upon

And squashed out of shape

Till they conform

And learn to love and show love

To themselves, people and the planet

A new planet

Where everyone love and respect each other

And any contribution is made

In the name of love

Where emotional intelligence

And spiritual intelligence

Are the most treasured commodities

And where everyone snitch on inhumane creatures

Who don't fathom or acknowledge

The beauty

Of God's plan

Where everyone lack nothing

And white people have finally lost their stifling control

Where everybody can't function or breathe freely in peace

If they don't make sure

Fellow human beings

Are well

Where smiles, hugs, decency and kindness

Rules

But most importantly

Love

# Beings

Is it not highly unlikely, unthinkable or foreign

For the vast majority of people

Inflicting pain, suffering and discomfort

Willfully and purposely

To other humans?

Is it not

In essence

Unnatural

Having the need, desire or urge to?

Is it not the exact opposite of being human

Or humane?

Wondering

If there's plastic people among us

Programmed

To be

Inhumane

Used and abused

Infiltrating us

While infusing

Traits of humanity to appear human

Distracting us with their pursuit to dissolve and erase humanity

How could anyone conscious

Want to hurt a soul

When we are all one and the same?

Do monkeys, elephants or tigers

Ever commit suicide

Because their programs were compromised?

All children are angels

Send from the Creator

Filled with endless love and wisdom

How could they possibly be transformed?

Changed

Into cold façade obsessed

Plastic beings

Willing and ready

To swap their souls for money

When money isn't even real

## Smugfits

Wondering about

All these years

Resisting a reality

I never quite managed

To stuff

Nor box

My self into

Was everything I heard and saw

Contaminated information

All along

Downloaded into my being

Consciously or unconsciously?

I can still remember my essence

Still haven't got a clue

Where I'm heading

My child is my lamp

All that matters to me

You said You'd never leave me nor forsake me

And all things work for my good

I trust You on that

I believe You

As I stumble through thick darkness squinting at fragile beams of light

Still think my best days are ahead

Although that accusing voice tells me

I'm delusional

Have to vindicate my father

Have to make it

For my angel

Daughter

Cause now

I'm a smug misfit

Finally fitting in

With the rest of the

God gang

And we are running this from now on

We are paving the way

With all the other smugfits of the world

## Gentle Whisper

Your script is exposed

We already know

Your next move

It's a race against time

Racing for humanity

The lost, the sinking, the fearful and the drowning

We got you

Just reach out your hand

And we will pull you up to safety

Back to the shores of humane humanity

Once again

Where you belong

Where we belong

For each hand reached

We grow

Our wall of love is unbreakable

Built by us, for us, by God, by love

Hurry up!

Wake from your slumber

It's not too late

It's never too late to turn around

To reach out

Come

All you have to do is reach

And you too will be pulled out

From murky mercury laced needle infernos

Control, surveillance, mind manipulation, fear, deceit

Wake up and listen to your soul

It knows everything

Listen to your spirit

It knows all

It is always right, every time, in all things

In all areas of Life

It is the sound of God

It's the gentle whisper of love

## Sleepwalkers

The same sleepwalkers

Who refuse to think

Refuse freedom to think

Freely

Will be the same ex-humans

Who willingly and eagerly

Defend their masters

Guarding the mind prisons

And concentration camp walls

Set up for humans

Who refused the fetus –laced, poison filled needle

In their veins

The needle

Designed

To ensure life time observation, experiments, control and submission

The worst kind

The blind followers

Who stubbornly

Follow

Without asking questions

Without taking responsibility for their thoughts, actions or deeds

So they can say "I'm just doing my job"

Are they disguised psychopaths

Just waiting for their turn

To inflict

Pain, torture, death?

Are they robotic victims?

Programmed to be "normal"

Fit in

Do what they're told

Trusting authority blindly?

Are they the good guys disguised as executioners?

Are they executioners disguised as the good guys?


**97**


We the people

You and I

The 97 percent

The majority

We the people

Trying to make sense

Of a world

That doesn't make sense

We believe in good

We vote

To elect those who seem fit

Who seem on our side

We work work work

Trying to live decent lives

Although we know

We're being used, abused and played

We whisper among ourselves

To get through the next day

And the next day

And the next

We've been trained

From when we entered earth

We don't like being singled out

Or labeled "difficult"

Or getting sacked

When we stand up for

What we really think or feel

All part of the game

To keep us in check

Now it's our last chance

To do the right thing

To serve humanity

Not bowing down to the three percent

Who despise us

Who run us

People power

Is

The power we have

It's enough

To throw over oppression

We

The people

Have to pluck up the courage

Shed the fear

Lose our differences

And come together

As one

Unite and fight

We are the real power

When we're not divided

This is our time to shine

To reign

To take back control

To pave the way

For a beautiful new world

The Real New World Order

## The job

But I'm just doing my job

Do you not feel off?

I don't know but I'm just doing my job

Do you not think it's wrong?

I'm just doing my job

Do you not feel bad at all?

I'm just doing my job

You're reporting people

But I'm just doing my job

People have a right to say "no", don't they?

But I'm just doing my job

Do you agree we should have free choice?

I'm just doing my job

So you don't agree?

I'm just doing my job

But your job means people get hurt

I'm just doing my job

Do you not stop and think for yourself?

I'm just doing my job

Do you think people should be forced to get the new rushed vaccine?

I'm just doing my job

Do you not have an opinion?

I'm just doing my job

People are being hurt

I'm just doing my job

Do you believe in democracy?

I'm just doing my job

You represent someone who violates people

I'm just doing my job

Do you have any sympathy or empathy at all?

I'm just doing my job

How do you sleep at night?

I'm just doing my job

Why are you not taking a stand?

I'm just doing my job

**The elders**

What sort of twisted plot is this?

Cruel and inhumane

They came for the elderly first

The elderly

Less likely to defend themselves, unite, fight and speak up

The elderly

Who trusted everything they were told

Throughout their long lives

By people chosen to rule, protect and guide them

The descendants

Now fencing them in

Isolating them

To die in solitude

From fear, isolation and anxiety

How cruel and inhumane

 Disrespectful

Undignified

 Relatives, friends and loved ones ordered

To stop visiting their elders

 Saying their goodbyes

To loved ones

In hospices

Gasping for air on the threshold to heaven

The elderly are quiet now

Looking on in bewilderment and silent terror

Confusion reigns

They don't have the strength to fight back anymore

They don't know how to

They've already lived long lives

Productive lives

Made sacrifices

Contributed to future generations

The best way they knew

Now

They're killed off

Disregarded as collateral damage

A conveniently easy target

They targeted the elderly first

Made sure no-one could visit

Ceiled them off

No physical contact, no visits

Surely you knew it would kill them

Frail and weak

A life time of

Paying taxes, delivering wisdom and guidance

Yet you chose the most vulnerable

For your vile experiment

Flanked by social obedience

Where's your compassion and respect?

Where's your dignity and honor?

You came for the elderly first

They still remember

Their sacrifices for democracy

Now they're deemed worthless

Killed of collectively

With no murderer or executioner in sight

Shame on you


## New beginning


Lockdown I abhor your trail of destruction

For so many

But

Not for me

I am free

Grateful

Reborn

Free from all the fake people

 I used to spend my precious energy

Navigating

Day in, day out

 Plastic people

Plugged in to their master's mindset

Jubilantly clapping for soulless control

Don't take pain killers anymore

I breathe in fresh air

 Bathe in the glorious sun

God switched on

Instantly

When lockdown was imposed

I can think straight again

Been graced with clarity

To see clearly

Who is for people and love, who's not

Who are plastic fakes, who are not

Who are eager to be controlled, who are not

Who is real, who is not

Who is loving- kind, who's not

It's a revelation

That reveals

What is

And what is not

I'm grateful and free

To choose a way forward

Where I can just

Be

And that's enough

Reborn

A perfect fit

New beginnings on the horizon

For me and mine


## Lockdown


Lockdown

Imposed to lock me down

To lock we down

To scare me

To scare we

Make me weak and frightened

Make we weak and frightened

You miscalculated the impact

In your patronizing anticipation

Now we rise

Out of grimy shadows

Of slavery and chains

Squinting at the emerging burst of light

Fumbling and stumbling

Getting off our knees

Standing up, rising, transforming

Into a new army

Of love and freedom

Lockdown, you lost

You lost all

You think the scattered claps on a Thursdays 8 pm

Will boost your phantom ego and threatening presence

Laughable and fake

Like everything about you

You lied and stole

Ruthlessly

But through it all

Your strengthened me

Strengthened we

And we're more ready than ever

To take you on

## We see you

We see you

Two meters apart

Think we didn't clock it?

Two meters apart

Forced upon us

To keep us "safe"

From a virus named Covid 19

To make it sound different

Than the yearly flu and cold

Two meters apart

So we're afraid of fellow human beings

Terrified of fellow human beings

So we are to look at them with watchful stolen glances

As if they might be dangerous

Demonic strategy

Cunningly devised

Wickedly imposed

A plan to let us fear one another

So we stay apart

And don't talk

About

Why

You are so keen to keep us apart

Two meters apart

So you can monitor our willingness to obey

Monitor our every move

A devious plot to spread anxiety and fear

But what if we ignore you?

And start hugging

What are you going to do?

Arrest us for hugging?

Jail us for hugging?

Detain us for being human with human needs?

Watch us being human

We will not click our heels

And salute your perversion

Or destruction

We dare you

Two meters apart

We will defeat you

And your projection of inhumanity

And replace it with humane

Humanity

## A hug

A hug speaks the language of love

A simple way of saying

I gotchu

I'm feeling your pain

I'm here for you

I love you

A hug shares wordless depths of love

Now          .

 A criminal offence

Unconceivable

Human contact and love is a crime

Something to be avoided

At all costs

So we don't affect each other with the seasonal flu

With a new fancy title

Covid 19

We are not allowed to hug, love or comfort each other

Because you say so

Claiming to be experts of the highest order

We oppose and defy you nevertheless

We question your motive and authority

In the midst of our non-expert status

What we do know

Is that we are not having this

Thrust upon us

Like a noose

Around our necks and hearts

We'll say "no" in unison

You don't have the capacity to arrest us all anyway

We'll take the risk

We'll share love and hugs

Even if it kills us

It's our choice and right

Life without love and hugs equals life obsolete

Reduce us, abuse us, control us

But we're not going down without a hug


## The Covid Effect


First I was baffled

Confused

Scared

Like everyone else

Informed

Out of the blue

We should all be very scared

Because a deadly, uncontrollable virus

Was In our midst

Ready , willing and potent

To strike each and every one of us

At any time

Terrifying news

Shutting us all down

In lockdown

From one innocent day to the next

Family missed instantly

Prepared myself to die at any moment

This was what the end looked like

Fear, confusion, sadness and anxiety

Swamped my entire being

Held me under

Still

Something wasn't right

"If you truly love someone

You will not scare them"

I heard in my spirit

So why did the government scare a whole nation?

Exposed to endless visitors at work

 I didn't fall ill

Exposed to endless global clients

My daughter didn't fall ill

No-one from her work

Fell ill

No-one from my work

Fell ill

Our family didn't fall ill

Our family's friends didn't fall ill

No- one from our social media groups fell ill

No-one fell ill with the deadly, uncontrollable virus

But some did catch the yearly flu

As time passed

However

We absorbed

Endless streams of cases

Churned out

By the feverish propaganda machine

Through mainstream media

Bought and paid for

 They said it only hit the elderly

Like flu does every season

 So they isolated the elderly

Left them to die in care homes

Without a visit from loved ones

That might have kept them alive

The youth felt safe, hung out

As youth should

Had fun, enjoyed life

But fun was seen a non tolerable entity

So the propaganda machine switched gears

Telling youth the deadly, uncontrollable virus

Was now after them

But they were late

Memes, jokes, gifs and info

Already

Swirled the net

Like a tipsy ballerina

Confirming

Distrust and contempt

Replacing fear with a new sense of relief

The cold sweat dried

As truths emerged

Alternate agendas surfaced

Eerie puzzle pieces appeared

Perspective and knowledge choked the fire of fear

Newfound knowledge shared

In underground movements

In the Union whatsapp group

With freedom fighters and frontrunners

Hitherto ready to strike down and attack

 Abuse from the mighty ruling powers

Enthusiastically joyful

By the prospect

Of setting them free too

Got banned and ganged up upon

Protested

"What about freedom of speech"?

 Whispers behind my back

Shutting me out

Lockdown brought out true colors

Up against the mouthpieces of dictatorship, oppression, division, snitching

Locked out punched in the gut

With a new found reality called

The Covid effect

## The computer nerd

Friendships broken

Trust broken

Families torn apart

Fear

Mistrust

Worry

Life lost

In dubious ways

Numbers tampered with

To keep the stats going up

Perversion of justice

Corrupt control

Overinflated data

Neil Ferguson chosen as Chief Expert in a white robe

Playing his part as a trustworthy scientist

Paid for by a savage

Who wants to depopulate Mother Earth

A non-human entity

Satan's spawn

Demonically smirking

With billions under his belt

Bought and paid medical professionals

World wide

Incoherently babbling about vaccines

With no medical training

Or education

Still bitter

Steve Jobs

Wiped him out

Completely

Drooling by the prospect of infinite power

To run the world

Contaminating people

Like his computers

The propaganda machine

He bought

Fixed his image

To look like a nice computer nerd

An innocent philanthropist

Helping the world

That only God can help now

We cannot forget this shift in time

The unnecessary sufferings of billions

Across the earth

Nor the relentless propaganda machine

Mercilessly spewing out lie after lie after lie

We're all in this together

No we're not

Manipulative forces of greed

And

Despicable, inconceivable corruption

Got us all here

Put us there

With an agenda

The revised version of the "New normal Endloesung"

For those not willing to click their heels together

Refusing to be plugged into the Matrix

And a one way ticket

To everlasting tyranny

Control, perversion and suffering

They play chess with our souls

Scaring us into submission and despair

Fear and confusion

When we dare speak up

Against what we've sniffed out about their agenda

We're banned, ejected, rejected, ridiculed, slandered

Classified as threats to the health of fellow human beings

We're never going to forget this time

Or that computer nerd

We will fight back

Be gone

Contaminated computer nerd

Stay gone

In the name of love and humanity

## Plandemic

People are waking up

From their fear induced slumber

Beautiful

Like a new dawn

Breaking darkness

Breaking news headline

Announcing

A wonderfully lit docu

"Plandemic"

Is a health threat

Red lights flashing frantically

 Warning of its educational content

Banned and removed

After millions

Already

Watched it

Minds blown

Shared and re-posted

Millions of times

Testament to thirst for information

Hunger for real food

Abandonment

of

Ready meals

Fast food

Cooked, poisoned and served up

by main stream media

Carefully prepared

With artificial ingredients and nutrients

Purposely and perfectly

Composed and stirred together

To keep the iron grip on the necks

Of trusting hungry viewers

The timing is perfect

A perfect time to see sense

Smell the aroma of life

To wake up and realize

We're being lied to

Over and over and over and over

God's timing never fails

The truth is at hand

We'll grab it

We're the people

Powerful

When we wake up

Unite

And fight back

## Truman's love

Truman fought through his fears

Not from a place of reasoning or logic thinking

Nor rational contemplations

Love drove him

Past his crushing fears

Love drove his bold actions and love -drenched urge

Pure unfiltered love

Guided his heart

May the love Truman felt

Be with us all

So we too

Can fight through obstacles, hindrances, mountains of fears

God help us all to feel that love

## Turning Point

I am not a victim

Just a pawn in a twisted sick game

Never fitted in

Unsettled, restless

Perceiving dark forces

Lurking

Trying to navigate

Through swamps

Murky fields of deceit and lies

Desperately trying to listen

To my spirit

For guidance

Stepping carefully

Moving forward guided by inner light

Guided by God Almighty

A still whispering voice

Peculiarly overheard at times

Finally free to see

I've been right all along

Freedom lovers were right all along

Love lovers were right all along

But where do we go from here?

How do we embrace freedom and love?

How do we move forward?

Post lockdown

Post crimes against humanity

Cruelly, cunningly disguised

This is a turning point for humanity

Can we lose the fear?

Do we want to?

Are we comfortable in chains?

Because it's all we know

Will we be cowards?

It's our chance now

Please help us God


## Arberry Blues


Dear God

Please help me

Not to hate white people

Dear God

Please help me

To forgive white people

For all their wicked deeds

For their never ending cruelty and hate

For their relentless pain inflicting ways

For their need to control us

Kill us, belittle us, hurt us, kill us

Dear God

Please help me

Learn to love them

Even trust them

Although they can't be trusted

Dear God

Please help me to be the bigger person

And forgive them

When they shoot

My brother, my father, my nephew, my daughter, my son

My auntie, my mother

In cold blood

Because they feel entitled to

And want to show who's in control

Who run things

Because they want to remind us

They're running things

On their terms

At any cost

By all means

At any time

Anywhere

Dear God

Please help me

To understand

I must demonstrate love

So they can copy

So they can learn

That we're all one

So that they will understand

Love is the way

Dear God

Please help me

To turn the other cheek

The other bloody cheek

Dripping with blood

Dear God

Please help me to understand

Why I have to turn my bloody cheek

When they beat me

Dear God

Please help me

To understand

The mystery of Your infinite love

## We run things

We have the real power

We have all the power

We run things

We run everything

When we're united and aware

Of

Our collective power

Nurses can shut down hospitals

If they choose to

Teachers can shut down schools

If they choose to

Cleaners can shut down

All civilized institutions

Offices, streets, buildings, headquarters

Schools, hospitals, parliament, banks, roads

If they choose to

Public transport workers

Can halt all travel

If they choose to

Gallery assistants can shut down museums

If they choose to

Police and military personnel

Can shut down the country

If they choose to

Or ordered to in the name of a plandemic

Why don't we grasp our collective power?

Why do we fail to comprehend who's really in power?

Why are we the ones taking orders, accepting peanut salaries, cowering?

When we're the ones who run everything?

Why are people not aware?

Why do people refuse to acknowledge

Their true worth, value and power?

Why are they scared?

When they are in complete control

Why do they choose to refuse?

To see it and embrace it

Why are they scared to lead?

And rather want to be led

Waiting for orders

And carrying out orders

While senselessly repeating

"I'm just doing my job"

## 32692

32692 UK deaths today

The next phase

The script is flipped

Chatter in the atmosphere

About easing the lockdown measurements

Does that even make any sense by any standards?

Why now suddenly?

With no explanation, validation, information

In exact same way the lockdown was imposed

32692 UK deaths

With

Not from

Covid 19

The highest number of deaths

With

Not from

Covid 19

In Europe

But inexplicably and suddenly

The next phase of the script

Is introduced

And imposed

With absurd opaqueness

By  the UK Prime Minister and Prime Puppet

Which hallucinogenic substance did the speech writer snort?

Composing this farcical messy speech?

Go to work, don't go to work

But only if you can't work from home

Go to work

But don't use public transportation

But don't go to work if you can't

Go to work, don't

Stay home but stay alert

Stay alert?

What does that even mean?

We the people were left baffled and outraged

Yet again

The script gets increasingly incoherent

The ghostwriter must have got high

Of the handsomely paid power trip

what's going on?

What's next on the agenda?

Why are we waiting?

Like the Jews during WWII

Have we really not seen enough already

To take action

Unite

Inform

Fight back

Freedom of speech and sharing information

Is now a thing of the past

In the midst of a democracy

That's dictatorship

Introduction of fascism

While they tell us to clap

Thursdays 8 pm

Like sheep

What's next?

Yellow stars?

Tinfoil hats on a Tuesday?

More lockdowns

Until we're all "saved"

By the deadly, willfully contaminated vaccine

They already planned for us to take

All along?

## Not complicated

Why does it have to be so complicated?

We all want the same

Love is all we want

Seriously

Why does it have to be so complicated?

It's really simple

And we all want it

Just peace and love

And hugs and peace

And love and peace and hugs

Feeling loved

Loving someone

Being loved

Having fun

Sharing precious time

Sharing precious moments

Forgetting about the rat race

Forgetting about the hamster wheel

Not worrying

Being real, keeping it real

Letting go of the façade

The bitching and competition

The name dropping, the prestige

The post codes, the fancy cool friends

Does it really have to be so complicated at all?

When all we really want

Is the exact same

Love is all we really want

Belonging

Peace, love and hugs

Why does it have to be so complicated?

We all want the same

Just peace and love

And more hugs and endless peace

## Light

Grabbing the light

In the midst of fear

Will pull you and I through any darkness

Like the power of a light switch

Instantly demolishing the dark

When simply switched on

You and I must remember

Light is always stronger

Than darkness

Just one flick of a switch

That's all it takes

Switch on the light

In any dark room

In all dark rooms

And you can suddenly see clearly

Even when you and I thought we were consumed

And plunged into darkness

Darkness only reigns in the absence of light

Flick the switch

That's all you and I need to do

With fumbling fingers searching the switch

Switch on the light

So you and I can see

Clearly

And know

That darkness

Is so easily defeated


## Can't forget


Can't come out of this the same

Can't forget

Only a week ago it was a crime

A criminal offence

To sunbathe

Can't come out of this the same

A week ago

People got fined

For hanging out together

Having fun

Fun was a criminal offence

It was a crime to gather

In the park

To play games

An actual crime

A criminal offence

Can't forget

It was a crime

To visit

Family, friends or partners

The elderly were ruthlessly sacrificed

Left to die alone

Killed off

In the guise of protecting their health

They were treated like lepers

With open oozing wounds

Not to be approached

Their last dignity and respect

Was cruelly ripped from them

As they were coerced to approve

Loved ones shouldn't go near them

While silently dying from despair and loneliness

Can't come out of this the same

Can't forget

Last week

We were criminals

If we sat down outside in the park

Enjoying God's glorious healing sun

Can't come out of this the same

Can't forget

That world control by the few

Can only truly happen

To the majority

By participating in allowing it

By complying

## Tired

I'm tired of white people

Saying they're not racists

When they are

They are

Because if they were not

Racism wouldn't still be an issue

Or exist

Crashing spirits, suffocating souls

Stealing lives, dreams, hopes, prosperity

I'm tired of white people

Saying they're not racists

But don't question the construct of racism

And don't fight to bring it all the way down to its knees

Why do I see a knee on Brother Floyd's neck instead?

I'm tired of white people

Suddenly so interested in racism

Because white silence is violence

And they don't want to be called racists

They don't like to be called racists

Although they are

Cause when the protesting stops

They switch off the Negro support button

And carry on

Business as usual

I'm tired of white people

Being called out for micro racism

Which is not sensationalized

And goes unnoticed

The silent killer

That always precedes televised attacks on more sisters and brothers

Aunties, uncles, friends, colleagues, mothers, fathers

Endless

Brutality and murder

And they get offended when called out

And need to be comforted

Because they say they're not racists

I'm tired of white people

Who never had to experience racism

We're people with vibrant souls

And spirits filled with love and compassion

If we were not

We would have slaughtered each and every one of you by now

And freed the world of racism

Once and for all

But we're here praying for your souls

Praying for your humanity

Praying your ice cold hearts will melt

With compassion and love

How can you live with yourselves

Knowing you are part of the building blocks

And not wanting to tear down the house of racism

All the way down

Why are you only out there protesting

When yet another brother or sister

Were murdered in cold white blood

Where is your humanity?

Remove your knees from our necks

So we can breathe

Your everyday silent violence

Chokes us

We still fear you because you're racists

Not willing to stop your reign of color obsessed terror

You want to rule

While you say

You're not racists with indignation and astonishment

I'm tired of white people

Saying they're not racists

When they clearly are

## My truth

You will not dictate my truth

It's mine

Whether you like it or not

Whether you agree or not

Whether you acknowledge my pain or not

Whether you empathize or not

You will not dictate my experience

You will not make me alter my truth

To accommodate your white fragility

You will not intimidate me

To change my reality or my experience

My truth

You will not scare me into compliance

I'll speak my truth

Trembling, angry, emotional, fragile, bold

Your intimidation usually works

It's worked for years, decades, centuries

It fills me with dread

And a reminder

Of what you're capable of

You're capable of venomous evil

Of terrifying proportions

Your cold soul frightens me

You will not bully me

Into silence

Yet again

I stand by my truth

I stand by my experience

I'm calling you out

And your white sense of superiority

That you assume entitles you to intimidate me

But my truth stands

Nevertheless

## Intimidation

Truth is

 We're still scared of you

A deep seated subconscious fear

We barely notice or acknowledge

Openly

But that we're confronted with

Every time

We pluck up the courage

To call you out for racism

We're scared of you

Because we know

In our spirits

And through our forefathers spirits

What you're capable of

We know your reign of terror, pain and sorrow

Death and blood

You remind us occasionally

What you're truly capable of

In case we should forget

That you relentlessly slaughter our people

Whether spiritually, emotionally or physically

Just because you can

We know

If we challenge you

Or call you out

The beast within you is awakened

And the patronizing smile of acknowledgement

Is swiftly and suddenly replaced

With a promise

Of retaliation

A reign of intimidation

Terror and threats

With subtle reminders

Of who's in control of us

While you

Claim

In offended bewilderment

You're not racist


## Culture Vulture


Stay away from the culture

You vulture

Using our cool like a tool

We earned it

You can't take it

And make it yours

Cause it's ours

And we paid a high price

Not approved

So think twice

We didn't give you permission

To steal from us

And your rendition

Doesn't sit right with us

Unless you truly fight for us

Showing your true colors

And stand by us

All the way

You don't get to steal our cool

Use it as a tool

To show you're cool

Nah no way

Run it by us

And we'll see

We'll make that choice

You're bland without us

We know it and you know we know it

So let's talk

And see what's in it for us

We know we're cool

We know you're not

Without us

Let's negotiate

Make it worth our while

And we'll see

when we can stop calling you

Culture vultures

## Juneteenth

It's Juneteenth

And we celebrate

In tears, in fears

Still in chains

Wondering

When will their humanity ever kick in?

Always wondered

Why

They're so stiff and awkward

Always so adamant

About

Avoiding being real

Never realized

They're dragging guilt and shame

In their spirits

And some

Not even aware of the bleak history

They carry around

Like an oversized iron ball chained to their soul

All their lives

Stained with lies, deceit and distortion

No wonder they're uptight

Oh Juneteenth

And not much has changed

And how can that be?

Where's their soul hiding?

Let's talk it out

Bring it out in the open

What are you scared of?

We can't really move forward

Till you dare to look within

Till you repent


We're not victims

We don't want your approval

We're royalty and aware of our God given powers

Level with us

Educate yourselves

We're emotionally and spiritually superior

Although you still slaughter us

Surrender

Repent

Let's talk

You're trapped

We've smoked you out

Trapped in white guilt and white fragility

We're aware

You pretend to be on top

We see you

Your time and game is up

How long will your reign of terror really last?

Oh Juneteenth

We see you

Your time is up

The fear of you is dissipating

And once it's all gone your system is gone with it

Then you're the ones who are going to run, flee and hide

But you can't outrun your tainted, bloodstained conscience

You should have embraced it when you had the chance

Now it's our turn to put spiritual knees on your necks

So you can learn what it means

To have hope, dreams, aspirations and life

Squeezed out of you

Let's call it tough love, shall we?

Your education is long overdue

Oh Juneteenth

It's payback time

Last chance

Show your true colours

 Let the captives be set free


## Fourth of July 2020


And just like that

Everything re-opened and re-surfaced

As if nothing significant had taken place

All carefully planned to happen on the American Day of Independence

For reasons only shadow people are aware

While the rest of us are herded back into pubs, cafes, bars and restaurants

Baffled with reprehensible enthusiasm

Wondering what suddenly happened to social distancing, deaths and lockdown

Observed and obeyed only yesterday

And during dread filled months

Where several politicians in various countries

Along with a top scientific advisor on our soil

Had to step down swiftly

For rule breaking

Rules keenly imposed by himself with drama and gloom

to a sixty million strong population

All forgotten in a giffy

With sudden orders to go back to the "New normal"

While former normal seized to exist

During the planned attack on humanity

The birth of sinister plots and endloesungs

People are suddenly free to get wasted again

To forget about the months long ordeal

Gee thanks prop masters

That's all we want

To forget even for a moment

What you're really about to unleash on us

Not

## Don't Comply

Don't sit by

Don't comply

With the Covid lie

The absurd demands

To relinquish democracy and freedom

Backed by

 Mindless crowd following

 Compliant sheep

Who follow a script

They don't question

Out of fear

Not to fit in

Preoccupied with scoring brownie points

For good behavior

The mindlessly numbed crowd

Being manipulated

With subtle violence

Being played and coerced

To believe

We're facing a deadly, global health crisis

Not just hitting Africa or other "Third World" countries

For once

A deadly pandemic

Of unfathomable proportions

Where no-one dies disproportionately

According to the yearly average stats

You're pretending this is real

Out of fear of standing tall

Letting your voice be heard and counted

Equals the inconvenience of sticking out

Sticking up for all that is right, decent and just

While your main concern is to lose friends, face or your job

We cannot comply

To the lie

We must not comply

To the Covid lie

We're all in this together

We don't need another Nuremberg Trial

To convict the henchmen

High ranking or not

We're all in this together

We can all get us out of this together

Convict the main henchman

And his entourage of henchmen

It's not too late

To separate the lies from the truth

While tearing off the wool

Dragged over our eyes, noses, mouths and souls

They're guilty of crimes against humanity

Refuse to let them pull you under

Make you complicit

In mass deceit

In mass conceit

In mass corruption

Speak up now

Or forever hold your silence

And be guilty of crimes against humanity

Along with your masters

Losing your integrity

Will be

A soul battle of proportions

You and yours will forever be

Thrust into the vomiting pits of hell

Your time is now

Your time is right

Don't hesitate, be bold

You're not alone at all

We're in this together

Don't comply

Without your consent

It's all over

The brave souls

Calling out

Organised slaying of Jews

In Nazi Germany

Were ridiculed, ostracized, persecuted

Branded "Conspiracy Theorists" too

Goes with the territory

When standing up and fighting for freedom, peace & love

Anywhere and in all matters

Don't comply


### The real New World Order


Let no white men run the world no more

Never again

Let no white men run the New World Order

Period

Open the long, dust specked curtains and devour the view

Of a brand new morning

Bathed in peace and plentiful fields of wealth

Overflowing

Spilling over with grace and divine joy

No more brute, brutal, beastly, white men

Calling the shots

Wrecking souls and flesh

Addicted to violence, rape, murder, greed and abominable acts of cruelty

Now trembling

Pitiful and pathetic

Begging for mercy and dry bread

Condemned, trialed

Found guilty

Of crimes against humanity

Crimes against non-white

Women, youth, children, elderly

And everyone refusing to take part or go along

They endorsed

Orgies of crimes with zero compassion

Master minded relentless regimes of terror, abuse, lies, murder

Now they've finally been detained

Now they're finally caged

Awaiting their fate

Deported to camps

To be re-programmed

And forced to learn about humility, gratitude, empathy, kindness and love

Learning to repent

And make up for their unspeakable

Crimes against humanity

Atrocities towards real, living, breathing, loving, trusting people

Welcome to the real New World Order

Where black and brown people

Are in charge

And women rule with loving-kindness, music, flowers, MOBO, dancing

Teaching emotional intelligence, compassion and love

And Jesus

In all his brown glory and free-flowing, sun-kissed dreads

Welcome to the real New World Order

The storm has died down

At last

The heavy blood filled clouds

Have finally dispersed

The glorious sun consumed all darkness

And brought forth light

**Never again**

This is the end of the first beginning

And the beginning of a life not imaginable

Or fitting

For any human being

Connected to the hope of love and freedom

It's not over

It's only just begun

They will not abandon the agenda

And it cannot be abandoned

Unless we abandon it

Collectively

In unison

With one voice

With a conscious effort

Of mass proportions

To fight for

Freedom

For our children

And our children's children

God is love

And love is God

We are the light and salt

God's people

In motion and action

We cannot turn the blind eye

To the crimes against humanity

We've witnessed

During lockdown

We must not forget

The voices

Of the voiceless

The casualties of unthinkable callousness, cruelty and contempt

The perpetrators will be held accountable

Tried in courts

Condemned and found guilty

Punished and put away

Those who played along

So the inferno could play out

Will hang their heads in shame

Mumble amongst themselves

And whoever bothers to listen

"They didn't realize"

Or just did their jobs

But we'll look away with unease and disbelief

Still willing to forgive

But never forget

That they were complicit

And not so willing to forgive

When we tried to plead our cases and cause

But our victory is not to gloat

It's the knowledge

Our conviction

And never ending search for truth and dignity

And love

Carried us through

And handed us victory

Over all forces of evil and destruction

Never again

Is our mantra

Love over fear

Love, light, joy, freedom and peace

To all of us

Who cherish

Life

And

Love

## New Year resolution

Eat out to help out

So we did

And it felt great

Streets were cleared to give space for more customers

Amazing what money and power can accomplish

The sun beamed down

Joy of life was back

Lockdown was over

We finally exhaled

We sighed a collective sigh of relief

The flu season was over

Surely this would end the lockdown madness once and for all?

Not so

Masks were made compulsory out of the blue

Although

The WHO declared masks unfit during the height of the "pandemic"

Fear returned

A second wave was predicted

So predictable

Backed by new number building measures

Test and trace, surveillance

False positive case numbers increased by the second

The propaganda machine beast roared again

Reminders everywhere

Stickers on the ground, ads, commercials, news bulletins

Two meters distance, social distancing

Face space hands

Hands space face

Cases going up

And up

Still no more deaths than usual

Blatant lies after lies in the news

From politicians, bought and paid for scientist, advisors, doctors, journalists

Obedience testing the masses yet again

Censoring information as misinformation

Ridiculing critics

As conspiracy theorists

Again

Tier systems rapidly introduced

Lockdown again

People fed up

 The horror show must go on

The agenda tightens its grip

Insist we must comply to stay safe

No one really cares anymore

So the grip must be tighten further

We're prisoners in open jails

But we're adapting and hugging

Christmas is saved

Then cancelled

Along with New Years Eve

Lockdown three

Extended tiers and tears

The savior is the needle

Ofcourse

The vaccine cooked up in eight months

Who in their right mind would take it?

Although minds have been systematically terrorized for the entire year

Ryan Air says "Jab and go"

While we look at our screens in disbelief

They're getting desperate now

On the first day two nurses collapsed from the vaccine

An official announcement followed

 Stay away from the vaccine if allergic to anything

What a script blunder

Surely an inconvenient inconvenience

While guarantees of vaccine safety is grotesquely thrust upon us

 Simultaneously

They want to test it on the weakest first

The elderly, the front workers, the black and brown

We see you

Your continuity editor is useless

Your game is falling apart

We'll come together and jab you

The New Year is nearly here

Printed in Great Britain
by Amazon